CCSS Genre Expository

Essential Question
What makes different parts of the world different?

by Betsy Hebert

Have you ever seen the Rockies? That's what most people call the Rocky Mountains. The Rockies are part of a huge mountain range. They stretch from Alaska all the way down to New Mexico. That's a really long way!

The Rockies are 300 miles wide in some places. They are more than 3,000 miles long. Only the Andes Mountains in South America are longer.

The Rockies march up North America.

In the United States, the Rockies extend through several states in the western region. Part of the Rocky Mountains runs through Colorado. At Rocky Mountain National Park, you can get a close-up view of the mountains. You can learn what makes the mountains, and the park, so special.

KEY

Rocky Mountains

★ National Park

United States

Canada

Water

Jasper

Banff

Glacier

Yellowstone

Rocky Mountain

Pacific Ocean

Mexico

Several national parks are found in the Rockies.

The park is a good place to study three mountain **ecosystems**, or life zones. Each zone covers a different **elevation**, or height, on the mountains. The zones also have different plants, animals, and climates.

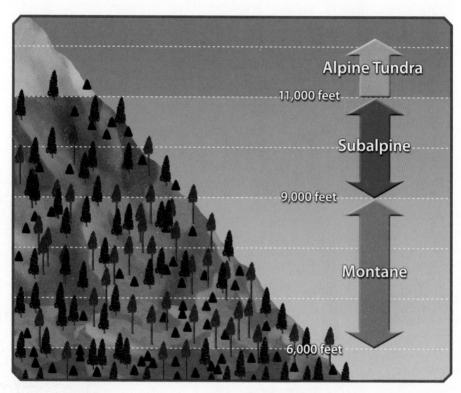

Alpine Tundra

11,000 feet

Subalpine

9,000 feet

Montane

6,000 feet

This shows the elevation range of each mountain life zone.

Fact
Rocky Mountain National Park was founded in 1915. It covers 415 square miles. It is a biosphere reserve, which means all the animals and plants in the park are protected.

Chapter 2

The Montane Zone

Let's take a closer look at the three life zones of Rocky Mountain National Park. We'll begin our study down low, at the bottom of the mountains.

This location is the montane life zone. The montane starts at about 6,000 feet above sea level. It continues up to about 9,000 feet.

These ponderosa pines thrive in the montane climate.

The montane is the most temperate of the life zones. Life is plentiful here. Tall ponderosa pines and Douglas fir trees grow here. They grow in groups called *stands.*

Aspen and willow trees grow next to fast-flowing streams. The leaves on the trees whisper and rustle in the breeze. Flowers and berries grow in wide meadows and on grassy hillsides.

When air gets colder in the fall, aspen leaves turn gold.

Many kinds of wildlife live in the montane ecosystem. Lively squirrels leap from tree to tree. They gather pine seeds to eat. Elk, moose, and mule deer graze in the meadows. Predators like coyotes and bobcats hunt mice and chipmunks. Eagles search for prey from the skies. They look for food to feed their young. Bluebirds and jays make nests, too. You can hear the birds calling.

This Abert's squirrel lives in the montane.

Chapter 3
The Subalpine Zone

Let's continue our journey. We'll move up higher into the mountains. The next life zone is the subalpine. *Sub-* means "below." *Alpine* means "very high." This is the middle zone. It is below the alpine zone.

The subalpine zone goes up to about 11,000 feet above sea level. The subalpine zone is darker and wetter than the montane. Thick forests of subalpine fir trees and Engelmann spruce trees curve up the mountain.

Subalpine forests are filled with Engelmann spruce trees.

At the highest edges of the subalpine, we come across eerie, twisted shapes. Believe it or not, these gnarled figures are trees. They are called krummholz trees.

Why do these trees look so strange? The winters are long and hard at this elevation. Strong, cold wind blows. The wind bends the spruce and fir trees. It changes their growth. The trees grow low and bent over. They are not straight and tall like trees lower down.

Krummholz trees can be centuries old.

The subalpine is home to a mixture of animals as well. Mule deer eat woody plants and grass. In spring and summer seasons, the deer find plenty to eat in the subalpine zone. Pine martens and bobcats also like this zone, and birds have plenty of nesting space in the forest. Juncos and chickadees are common.

Pine martens such as this one live in the subalpine zone.

Chapter 4
The Alpine Tundra

Let's keep climbing. We leave the forest and finally arrive at the third life zone. Now we are in the highest part of the park. This is the alpine **tundra** zone, which is above 11,000 feet.

The highest peaks in the park are in this zone. Dozens of these peaks are more than 12,000 feet high. To understand how high that is, think about airplanes. Airplanes fly at about 30,000 feet. These peaks are almost half as far up, so you know these are tall mountains!

Longs Peak rises to 14,255 feet and is the highest point in the park.

At first, the rocky slopes of the alpine zone look empty. We are above the **tree line** here, so no trees grow. Winds howl and snow falls most of the year in this harsh climate. But if you look closely, you'll see that the zone is not lifeless.

Tucked in close to the ground, some hardy plants and flowers grow and bloom. Many of the plants escape the fierce winds by growing low and small. Others are helped by their red color. The red plants change the sun's weak rays to make heat for themselves.

Alpine flowers give the bare ground a burst of color.

Photodisc/Getty Images

Small pikas can fit nicely under the rocks.

Only a few animals live in this frozen zone. Bighorn sheep are good climbers and use their skill to escape from predators. The sheep like the steep cliffs in the alpine. They spend most of their time in this zone.

Pikas and marmots live all year in the alpine. They make dens under the rocks. Ptarmigans are the only birds that live in the alpine all year. They don't mind the cold. They turn white in winter to blend in with the snow.

Fact
Only male bighorns have big, curved horns. During mating season, males use their horns to battle. They crash into each other headfirst. The noise from the crash echoes through the mountains.

It's been quite a journey! We've traveled through three different life zones of Rocky Mountain National Park. The park is home to hundreds of **species** of plants and animals. It is a unique and special place.

Many visitors use the hundreds of miles of hiking trails in the park.

Respond to Reading

Summarize

Use important details to help you summarize *Rocky Mountain National Park*. The diagram may help you.

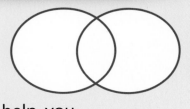

Text Evidence

1. How do you know *Rocky Mountain National Park* is expository text? GENRE

2. How is the montane zone like the alpine tundra zone? How is it different? Use details from the selection to support your answer. COMPARE AND CONTRAST

3. Use what you know about compound words to figure out the meaning of *wildlife* on page 7. COMPOUND WORDS

4. Write about how Rocky Mountain National Park is different from where you live. Use selection details to tell how they are the same and how they are different. WRITE ABOUT READING

Compare Texts
What makes Yellowstone a special part
of the Rocky Mountains?

Yellowstone

Yellowstone is another national park in the Rockies. It lies mostly in Wyoming and partly in Montana and Idaho.

Yellowstone has its own unique and special features. This park has more hot springs than any other place in the world.

Hot springs form when rain or melted snow flows onto magma, very hot rock below Earth's surface.

Geysers

Geysers are hot springs that **erupt**. They shoot hot water out like a fountain.

Yellowstone has more than 200 geysers. Some of the geysers send water more than 100 feet into the air.

Old Faithful, the most famous geyser in the park, erupts about every 90 minutes.

17

Mudpots

Mudpots are hot springs that do not have much water. The water that is in a mudpot breaks the rock down into clay.

The water and clay mixture turns into mud. Hot steam bubbles up through the layers of mud.

The gases in mudpots make them smell like rotten eggs!

Tony Waltham/Robert Harding World Imagery/Getty Images

Make Connections

What features make Yellowstone different from other parks? ESSENTIAL QUESTION

Would you prefer to visit Yellowstone National Park or Rocky Mountain National Park? Why?

TEXT TO TEXT

Glossary

ecosystem *(EK-oh-sis-tuhm)* all the plants and animals that live in a certain area *(page 4)*

elevation *(el-uh-VAY-shuhn)* the height of a place above sea level *(page 4)*

erupt *(i-RUPT)* to throw out matter, like water or lava, with force *(page 17)*

species *(SPEE-sheez)* a group into which plants and animals are divided based on shared traits *(page 14)*

tree line *(TREE lighn)* the start of the highest mountain areas where no trees can grow *(page 12)*

tundra *(TUN-druh)* an area with frozen ground and no trees *(page 11)*

Index

Focus
on
Science

Purpose To find out more about a special feature of Yellowstone or Rocky Mountain National Park

What to Do

Step 1 Choose something from the book that you would like to learn more about. For example, you might look up an animal, a plant, or a type of hot spring.

Step 2 Read more information about this topic. Share what you learn by making a poster or other display. Include a drawing and fun facts about your topic on your display.

Step 3 Present your display to the class.

Conclusion Tell why you chose the feature and why you think it is special.